KU-612-456

OUT OF ORDER

Compiled by Andrew Fusek Peters Illustrated by Clive Goodyer

Evans

EVANS BROTHERS LIMITED

Contents

OUT OF ORDER

Compiled by Andrew Fusek Peters **Illustrated by** Clive Goodyer

Francis Holland School

R17233

Published in 2009 by
Evans Brothers Limited
2A Portman Mansions
Chiltern Street
London W1U 6NR

© Evans Brothers Limited 2002

First published in 2002
This edition published in 2009

Printed and bound in the UK by
CPI Mackays, Chatham ME5 8TD

All rights reserved. No part of this publication may be re-
produced, stored in a retrieval system or transmitted in
any form, or by any means, electronic, mechanical,
photocopying, recording or otherwise, without the prior
permission of Evans Brothers Limited.

British Library Cataloguing in Publication Data
Out of Order
    1. Children's poetry, English
    I. Peters, Andrew, 1965
    821.9'14'08

    ISBN 978 0237 537 777

Editor: Su Swallow
Design: Simon Borrough
Production: Jenny Mulvanny

To Rudy Krejci

Lines

I must never daydream in schooltime.
I just love a daydream in Mayshine.
I must ever greydream in timeschool.
Why must others paydream in schoolway?
Just over highschool dismay lay.
Thrust over skydreams in cryschool.
Cry dust over drydreams in screamtime.
Dreamschool thirst first in dismayday.
Why lie for greyday in crimedream?
My time for dreamday is soontime.
In soontime must I daydream ever.
Never must I say dream in strifetime.
Cry dust over daydreams of lifetimes.
I must never daydream in schooltime.
In time I must daydream never.

Judith Nicholls

One Day In The Art Room

"...and when you've measured
your horizon find the vanishing
point **are you listening lad?**"
His voice ricochets shrapnel
down their ears, "...then join
your four corners put in the
telegraph poles a road get rid
of your guidelines thus and
now you've got perspective
any questions?"

And from the back a voice
Drops splashing into the silence:

"Eh Sir, did you rob them shoes
Off a tramp?"

Kevin McCann

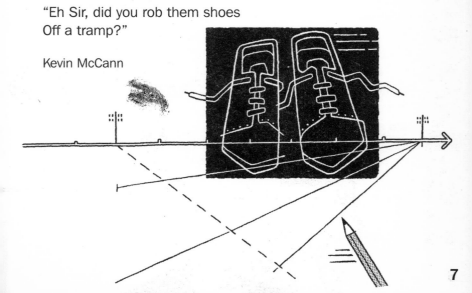

A Classroom

The day was wide and that whole room was wide,
The sun slanting across the desks, the dust
Of chalk rising. I was listening
As if for the first time,
As if I'd never heard our tongue before,
As if a music came alive for me.
And so it did upon the lift of language,
A battle poem, *Lepanto*. In my blood
The high call stirred and brimmed.
I was possessed yet coming for the first
Time into my own
Country of green and sunlight,
Place of harvest and waiting
Where the corn would never all be garnered but
Leave in the sun always at least one swathe.
So from a battle I learnt this healing peace,
Language a spell over the hungry dreams,
A password and a key. That day is still
Locked in my mind. When poetry is spoken
That door is opened and the light is shed,
The gold of language tongued and minted fresh.
And later I began to use my words,
Stared into verse within that classroom and
Was called at last only by kind inquiry
'How old are you?' 'Thirteen'
'You are a thinker'. More than thought it was
That caught me up excited, charged and changed,
Made ready for the next fine spell of words,
Locked into language with a golden key.

Elizabeth Jennings

The Minister For Exams

When I was a child I sat an exam.
The test was so simple
There was no way I could fail.

Q1.   Describe the taste of the moon.

It tastes like Creation I wrote,
it has the flavour of starlight.

Q2.   What colour is Love?

Love is the colour of the water a man
lost in the desert finds, I wrote.

Q3.   Why do snowflakes melt?

I wrote, they melt because they fall
onto the warm tongue of God.

There were other questions.
They were as simple.

I described the grief of Adam when he was expelled from Eden.
I wrote down the exact weight of an elephant's dream.

Yet today, many years later,
for my living I sweep the streets
or clean out the toilets of the fat hotels.

Why? Because constantly I failed my exams.
Why? Well, let me set a test.

Q1.   How large is a child's imagination?
Q2.   How shallow is the soul of the Minister for Exams?

Brian Patten

How Not To Pass GCSE Maths

Estimate the distance
From your front gate to school
And, given an average speed of 5 mph,
Calculate
The last possible moment
To get out of bed.

Roger Stevens

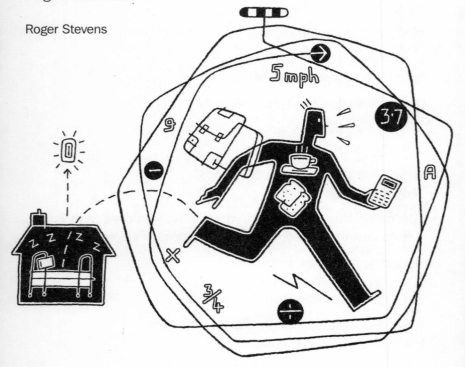

Arithmetic

She takes ten and divides it by three:
it breaks, hard-edged, echoing.

She divides a wet sky by a high window,
she wants to add a radio, take away the teacher.
The day isn't working out right.

She's given up caring about correct answers.
That makes the sums easy. So easy it bores her.

She measures the drawn-out length of the lesson
against the chipped edge of the desk - and still
finds it's too long till the bell.

She counts up her friends and subtracts
her enemies. Now that's interesting

but difficult, difficult.

Dave Calder

Kid Story

Let's set the scene - it was Halloween.
Hanging out in the rec, feeling blue
And bored out of our skulls, nothing to do:
Remembered Mr Rogers, for a dare,
Egged each other on to give him a scare.
Bought a bunch of eggs from the corner store,
With Halloween masks, we knocked on the door.
One of the gang screamed "Trick or Treat!"
Then we scrambled down the street,
But not before we managed to get
A 'Mr Rogers Omelette!'
He went ape, it was great for the crack,
The night we launched our egg attack.

It was just for fun, we're not that cruel,
But we haven't seen him since in school.
Just a tasteless little yolk,
Can't Mr Rogers take a joke?
Next time, no treat, we'll try the trick
Of smashing his windows with a brick.

Polly Peters

Mr Rogers

Too busy marking, I hadn't seen,
That once again it was Halloween.
Up all night, feeling blue,
Working in the living room, as you do.
You start to wonder *What's the point?*
I had reached my boiling point,
Twenty years, I've given this school,
I care about my kids, I must be a fool.
That night, quite late, the buzzer went,
Opened the door to my lads hell-bent
On treating me to their idea of a joke.
"Let's get the fat bloke!"
They chanted as they chucked their eggs,
Then ran away as fast as their legs
Could carry them. Now, I'm a mess,
Suffering from stress related illness.
I couldn't face my class next day.
I ask you, what would I say?
Thanks to a single violent spell,
I've learned to hide inside my shell.

Polly Peters

Doing Time

Ignorance was no excuse they said so I was sent to school.
Fourteen years I got. I'm more than half way now
but it still feels like a life sentence.

School's tough.
I've seen innocent friends turned into swots
well on their way to becoming hardened students.

There's little hope for those who get a thirst for knowledge.
Most will end up in and out of educational institutions all their lives.
But I'm smart – that won't happen to me – no way!

I'll keep my head down, keep my slate clean,
make sure the authorities don't notice me –
serve my time quietly

until that great day when I'm released
and can go straight out
and find myself an honest job.

Philip Waddell

Head Teacher's Wise Words

Our Head Teacher said

That dogs live short lives

Compared to humans

Because they move

From sleep to action

So quickly

I asked if that was also

True of cows

Because

It sounded

Like bullocks

To me

Roger Stevens

Too Much Like Hard Work

My square-eyed young nephew called Lee
Was given this book after tea;
He said to himself,
"It looks good on the shelf,
But now I'll go back to TV".

Mike Jubb

Jambo

Jambo playing football on the back field. His jeans rolled up to his knees covered in mud. Boots with no studs slipping and skidding. No-one watches except the tall cooling towers of the power station in the distance. No-one cheers him on.

But as soon as Jambo scores, he's floating across the turf of Wembley Stadium. The stray dog yapping at his heels that jumps up to lick his face is the team captain's bristly embrace. And the women on the landings in the block of flats behind are the crowds on the terraces, waving banners that aren't really wet sheets after all. Even the hard-faced kids skiving off school round the back of the burnt-out garages look like they might want to line up for his autograph.

Jambo punches the air as he climbs the railings to drag the ball out of a clump of nettles. He doesn't care. A goal is a goal, and when you score you're a winner - it doesn't matter where you are.

Dave Ward

Some People's Words

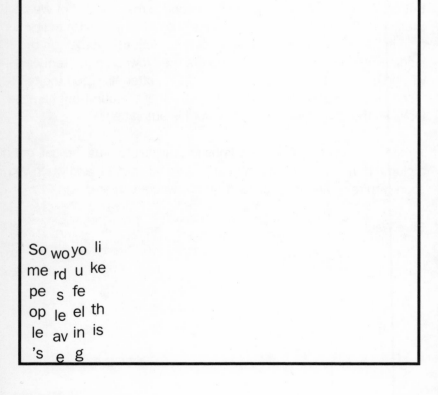

Some people's words leave you feeling like this

David Petts

Stammerer
(for Sir Alec Guinness)

Stammer. Yammer.
Stutter. Splutter.
Try as I might,
words won't come out.

Pushing. Blushing.
Rushing. Flushing.
'Don't pick on me!'
I long to shout.

Mumbling. Bumbling.
Fumbling. Stumbling.
That I have the answer
there's no doubt.

Rambling. Strangling.
Dangling. Jangling.
'Come on lad,
just spit it out!'

If I could, Sir
then I would, Sir.
Have you any idea
of what it's about?

Teenage years
of pain and fears,
a prisoner of
speechless rage.

What might you think
of me now, Sir,
as I earn my living
upon the stage;

the finest actor
of his age?

Jim Hatfield

Back At School

The kids all call me
Four Eyes
So my Dad says
Just ignore them
And my Mum says
Never mind babe,
Have some more cake...

So the kids all call me
Fat Guts
So my Dad says
Ah belt them one
And my Mum says
Never mind babe,
Have some more cake...

So now
The kids all call me
Spotty
So my Dad says
Oh fight your own battles
And my Mum says
Never mind babe,
Stay off if you like...

But I say
No thanks cos tomorrow
We've got English
And I might be fat
And I might be spotty
And I do wear glasses
But I can make up poems
And stories
And I'm sick of eating cake!

Kevin McCann

Quiet Kid On The Bus

Shrunk into myself
coat pulled tight
quiet kid on the bus
on a rainy night

Can't see my eyes
can't see my face
quiet kid on the bus
in my stinking space

Kids at school
all say I smell
quiet kid on the bus
in a sweating hell

on a rainy night
in my stinking space
quiet kid on the bus
can't see my face

Ian McMillan

Hateboarding

It was wheely great,
Taking off from concrete,
Arms wide as wings on a natural high.
At a cruising altitude of four inches above pavement level
We cruised homewards,
High jumping kerbs,
Sparking street edges.

Silent and twice our size
They sidled up to offer us a deal -
Your skates or a smash in the face.
We swerved and slalomed off
To avoid the brewing storm of hate,
But they were clouds,
Raining down on us with fists
'Till we went down in flames
and floods of tears. Now I was floored
They smiled as they hijacked
My much adored skateboard.

And on the tube, the adults did their best
As they do
To ignore the teenager
With a cut lip and his pride crushed,
Crash landed,
Never to soar again.

Andrew Fusek Peters

Cross Words

```
            t
t        wh am
r i p        r      d
i          a  twist          s  s  scrap
poke    s  h g  u        slang  h
   i   shout   grip    a  a    u
   b  claw   m   c      u  spit    c
wreck   e  pull      n  n   choke
h a   shake    o  s  c  a     h
a t   n  r       hurl  hurt
c   s  e   stab  t    i        l
k   wrench     i     n  j
   a    r    o   f  s  grab
   t   rave  flog   bang
   b    a  e      c       t
   a    n   knock   hit
scratch            let's
h                   be
                    e
                    s
            mates
```

Gina Douthwaite

The Game

I must tell you this:
there was a boy – Tommy Prentice.
The afternoon I'm thinking about
he stopped me with his shout
of just my first name,
all friendly-like – no blame,
jealousy, resentment or distrust –
telling me I must
come out with him now
and play – he had friends waiting, although
it was me they wanted: without me
the game was no good. OK?
Of course OK. Tommy Prentice
was tall, handsome, cool, use-
ful at fly-half, with slick black hair
fringeing his level stare.
And he wanted me? Like I say,
of course it was OK.

We found his friends
where the real garden ends,
or ended, rather, and the wild
began – wild as in where a child
might imagine the worst to lie
hidden in tall grass, in the poked-about eye
of a pond, in the fuzzy shade
a colossal cedar tree made
as it brooded above everything,
its green stratospheres tuned to sing
a thin sphere-music which never ends.

Back to those friends.
I cannot get clear
their names, height, number etc here -
only that none of them gave a sign,
not so much as one single frown
between them, of what was in store -
though maybe that had more
to do with accident than plan,
maybe (I'm sure if once he began
to explain, Tommy Prentice
would end up saying this)
it was my fault not theirs,
for being lippy, or having fair hair,
or somehow egging them on.

Neither can I say how the game began.
One minute we were standing around
glopping cones into that dead pond,
the next it was World War Two,
the Far East, I was a POW,
and they were the Japanese.
Ridiculous, everyone agrees,
if ever I tell them. Funny, even.
But for a child raised on the idea of Heaven
and God firmly installed there... .
You get the idea.
After that it was a rope and me
lashed to the cedar tree,
the puzzled bark (like elephant skin close
up) creasing my face,

my dungaree top yanked to my waist,
and my back bare lest
the Japanese, who now saw
a good chance of winning the war,
found it hard
to get at me under the guard
of thin air with their bamboo canes –
though since they did so again
and again, I should have said

difficulty was not something they had
much on their minds - certainly less
than I did, what with the mess
of blood starting to flip over
such clothes I still had as cover,
what with the tree
bark's now all consuming (to me)
fascination: the pale fawn skin,
the parched cracks leading the eye inside to softer and spice-scented darker wood,
and beyond that the sense I had
of pure blackness, where I might fall
out of myself entirely if I let go at all.

How long did that last?
All I can say is: it went past -
though having stepped so far out
(I mean in) to their work, they were not about
to make it seem like a mistake,
these boys, not something they might take
back, or think I didn't deserve.
They even held their nerve
when a teacher sauntered by,
a man who, noticing the tableaux

(six or so boys with canes
and one half undressed, in pain)
called out
'Everyone there fine?'
and made do with 'Right as rain,
Sir. Right as rain'
before he surged quietly away,
thick rubber-soled shoes making hay
with the grass he trampled as he went.

That's when I understood what it meant
to be as I had become:
dumb-struck, my voice whipped down the scale
from speech to whisper to whimper to wail
to nothing, as my spirit also sank
away from human into the frank
dependency of a creature
on more powerful natures.
When they eventually let me go
I still did not know
what to say except 'Thank you' -
softly, admittedly, but 'Thank you'
all the same -
leaving Tommy Prentice to some new game
under the impassive cedar tree,
tugging the top of my dungarees
gingerly up, my face bearing the mark
of corrugated bark -
fading, but still deep
as if I had just woken from sleep.

Andrew Motion

Ballad Of Matt The Knife

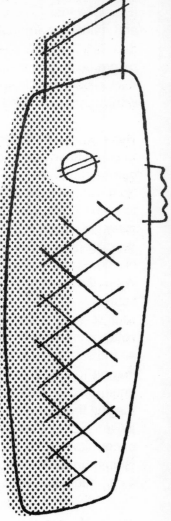

Why oh why did I carry a knife?
Because I was so scared for my life,
How I strutted the cruel school yard,
Bigger than the bully boys hard.

They beat me 'til I was blue and black,
My bloody nose and tooth for the crack.
But I'm a firework, watch me flare,
Now I wonder, will they dare?

Did I-did I-diddle-I-die,
Sharp as hate and clever as a lie.

Then there came, there came a day,
When we put childhood away,
Tattle taunts and treasure toys,
This is the moment, come on boys!

Light the match, and stand well back,
I'm fizzing, ready to attack.
Incandescent Roman Candle,
My revenge too hot to handle.

Did I-did I-diddle-I-die,
Sharp as hate and clever as a lie.

The fuse is lit and from each pocket,
Flies a silver bladed rocket,
Now you'll find out how I feel,
We circle like a Catherine wheel.

Bang like a banger! Dance, he's down,
I wear the victor's sparkling crown.
But what's this? I stagger in pain,
As from my chest flows golden rain.

Did I-did I-diddle-I-die,
Sharp as hate and clever as a lie.

Nothing sorted, nothing solved
The fun and fury has dissolved,
Watch me fall without a shout,
On the ground, I am burnt out.

This bloody ballad of the knife
That did not save but snatch my life
See my mother, father cry,
For their son, the bonfire guy.

Did I-did I-diddle-I-die,
Sharp as hate and clever as a lie.

Andrew Fusek Peters

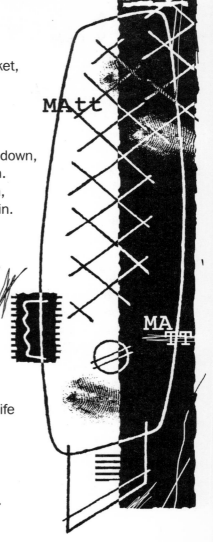

So Clever

My father was allergic to cleverness
and would come out in a rash
spate of domestic petty violence,
usually a slap round the head
suspected of containing the source of the cleverness.

Most times it would be for some smart answer
but other times it would come out of the grey:
the slap round the head and the "You think
you're so clever, don't you?"
and you would search whatever you'd just said or done
to find the trace particles of cleverness,
so that your future speech and actions
could be more cleverness-free.

All five of us might turn out at any moment
to accidentally contain cleverness
that had not been clearly labelled in our own minds;
and later I personally compounded the problem
with two "A" levels,
and even the one I failed was no mitigation,
for all time spent on study
was time wasted on cleverness;
and if he had known that I would grow up to get a degree
and write satirical poetry
he would certainly have told me
that I thought I was so clever, didn't I?
I thought I was so clever.

But all cleverness was bad cleverness
and the cleverest sort doubtless the worst of all.
How my dad would have hated to be Hermann Einstein
with the constant necessity
to slap little Albert round the head,
saying, "You think you're so clever, don't you?
You think you're so clever."

David Bateman

Family Break Up

F ILY

BREAK UP

SPL T

A ART

SEP   ATE

UNITS

NEW S ART

David Petts

If Only

If only I'd stayed up till four in the morning
and run through the dawn to watch the balloons
at the Festival ground,
and seen you as your balloon rose high
on a huff of flame, and you'd waved,
and a paper aeroplane had swooped to the ground
with your mobile number scrawled on the wings.

If only I'd known that you were crying
when you stood with your back to me
saying that it didn't matter
you'd be fine on your own.
If only I'd trusted your voice
instead of believing your words.

If only I hadn't been too late, too early,
too quick, too slow, too jealous and angry,
too eager to win
when it wasn't a game.
If only we could go back to then
and I could pick up your paper aeroplane
and call you for the very first time.

Helen Dunmore

Incendiary

That one small boy with a face like pallid cheese
And burnt-out little eyes could make a blaze
As brazen, fierce and huge, as red and gold
And zany yellow as the one that spoiled
Three thousand guineas' worth of property
And crops at Godwin's Farm on Saturday
Is frightening - as fact and metaphor:
An ordinary match intended for
The lighting of a pipe or kitchen fire
Misused may set a whole menagerie
Of flame-fanged tigers roaring hungrily.
And frightening, too, that one small boy should set
The sky on fire and choke the stars to heat
Such skinny limbs and such a little heart
Which would have been content with one warm kiss
Had there been anyone to offer this.

Vernon Scannell

My Mother

She is thin as a needle,
Weaving her way
In and out of sleep.
Forget food now,
Her hunger for life is done.
Too weak to sip from a straw,
She sucks on a sponge,
A little liquid for her lips
To whisper love in my ear.

She lies in the bed
She will not rise from,
As the illness sings in her body,
Dark harmonies.
Kidnapped by cancer,
There is no ransom big enough,
Except for the silver that pours from my eyes
And the vault of my heart,
Cracked
        As
            She
                Flies.

Polly Peters

Tidal Wave

And the fist is a threat
Like a cloud that's wet,
And the rain is a pain
That hasn't sunk in,
Yet.

It's a slippery punch that lands on the face;
Slap claps around his chops as a roar of thunder;
And the smile is sharp, a clean cut blade,
Slash, slice, the words carve cold like a piece of steak,
Eating at his pride. Going under,
The boy dives low, a dolphin snared in his father's net,
Struggle and squirm in the ultrasound,
Can't break free,
Yet.

Stand up, Stand up, a tower of nerves
Tremble in your father's wake
For my floundering mother's sake
Be strong as a reef, submerging grief
The tide isn't in,
Yet.

Class Poem, Y11-1, Stour Valley School,
Shipston

Bedtime Kiss

There was nowhere to hide,
No safety in silence.
A thrush can stab and skewer
The tender flesh
Inside the brittle shell,
Without pause or pity.
Yet at bedtime she would coil
Still as a snail in the shuddering dark
And listen for the soft slither of his hand
Along the landing wall.

Sometimes there was a breathless moment
When she thought he would not come.
Would unhook his hungry fingers from the banister
And turn away.
But he always came
Whispering his twisted words of comfort
As he explored her misery
Exposed her loneliness.
"You love your cuddles
Don't you?"

She did not betray him
Being powerless and afraid of fuss,
So she stored her grief like a secret
Until the last day of school
When she leaned over the stone bridge
And wept her fears into the brown water
Where other girls threw their berets.

Now, in the locked warmth of her student room,
She coils like a snail in the sheltering dark
And still she strains not to hear
The soft, soft slither of a far-away hand.
"You love your cuddles
Don't you?"

Sarah Dore

First Bra

Half way through my thirteenth year
They arrived.

While other girls stared mournfully
Down the fronts of their smooth school blouses,
My buttons battled against an invasion of
Unwanted,
Uncontainable,
Unstoppable swellings
That weighed me down with womanhood.

At first, I fought them.
Trapped them inside tight vests,
Refused to surrender my right
To tree-houses and playground slides
And the world of wrinkled socks.

But they strained and struggled,
Forcing their way to victory
Until there was only one bitter weapon left.
With cold fingers
I fixed the steely hooks
Of my first bra,
Encased my rebellious flesh in bonds
As white and unyielding as a straight jacket,
And just as inescapable.

Yet they still won.
Swung themselves free,
Stood proud and defiant
And inflated with triumph,
While my childish self
Was pressed to death
In a cruel, cotton cell.

Clare Bevan

Spots Are Cool!

We're so pretty. We're so zitty.
We're the spotty crew.
Bad skin's fab, so grab a scab
and an abscess or two.

We're the acne posse, the radical creatures.
We've got friendly wart-hog features.
Spots are trendy. Scabs are ace.
It's hip to be a pizza-face.
Yo! Acne's in. It's no disgrace.

Join the side
who eat with pride
anything that's been deep-fried.

Solve life simply: grow more pimply.
Give yourself a great big thrill:
chuck your tubes of Clearasil,
of Biactol and Oxy 10.
Join the loudly, proudly poxy men
and the badly blistered sisters.

So hit the street, carbuncle-feet,
and do your best to fester.
Yeah! Zit up, babe. Get 'em breeding.
Pop 'em. Squeeze 'em. Set 'em bleeding.

And, as you bust your pustules,
grease that skin. Block those pores.
You've got red 'n' yellow running sores.

Go psychedelic, crater-face.
You're the surface of a planet in outer space.
So scab up, dude. You're an awesome case.

Nick Toczek

Get The Text Message

Down the street, or in the park,
Hanging round 'til after dark,
like the sky, we're feeling blue
Drifting clouds with nothing to do.
Dawdle, gossip, blow the breeze
Sailing on the concrete seas:
Subjects? For the girls, it's boys,
And for the boys, the latest toys:
Text messaging likes, dislikes:
Roller blades, scooters, bikes.
Home is hell, too young for the pub
No bus that goes to the nearest youth club.
Neighbours shout that we're all thugs
Dropouts doing dangerous drugs:
And yeah, there's always one or two,
That doesn't sum up the whole of the crew:

Give us a place with internet,
Snooker, sounds, out of the wet,
We'd be home and dry and out of your hair,
"Sorry! No funding!" Does anyone care?
So now, they've made this mad curfew,
Punished us for nothing to do
No more hanging round the park,
Just jail our spirits after dark.

Polly Peters

A Real Case

Doubtful,
I have a fever
or any other measurable symptom.
I'm just down with a sniffly case
of sudden-self-loathing-syndrome.

TODAY!
It hit me like a thwop of mashed potatoes
snapped against a plate,
an unexpected extra serving
of just-for-now-self-hate.

Today, I'm worthless,
a leftover bath,
a wad of second-hand gum.
I belong in a twist-tied bag
with the rest of the toys that won't run.

My mood's as welcome as
incoming dog breath,
or a terminal case of split ends.
I sparkle like a dust rag,
I could attract mosquitos,
maybe not friends.

In fact, I could be contagious!
I'm a downer to say the least.
And if you try and
push my mood swing,
I'll only drag my feet.

Why? I couldn't tell you.
Just some days I get up and get down.
It's not a permanent disability, though.
Tomorrow,
I'll come around.

Sara Holbrook

Haiku

I was daydreaming
about being popular,
and it made me smile.

Mike Jubb

Fat

This is where it starts, she says,
pushing up the child-sized T-shirt,
teasing out the band of empty skin
where it lapses from the ribs.
Up to seven stone already
and only been eating a month.

She's hungry all the time, she says.
Hungry, or sick, or both.
Just like when she was… you know.
She swallows the word. Before
she took herself in hand, before
she lost eight stone in two years.

You'd be surprised, she says,
addressing my abdomen, my thighs,
how easy it is if you try.
It just drops off you. Her eyes slide shut
and her speech is sticky
from all the pills she takes to stop her crying.

She's going to see her boyfriend, she says.
They doubled the dose before they'd let her out.
He stood by her through thick and thin…
her head lolls. He'll go mad seeing her like this.
He hasn't touched her since they took her in
and all she wants to do is sleep.

They're scared she'll cut herself, she says,
lots of the girls do that. Not her.
She rolls back her sleeve to prove it.
The white flesh of her forearm is blued
with the violence of intravenous feeding.
Okay, she says, I went a bit too far.

Jean Sprackland

Leer Pressure

This is how to be a lad,
I learned it in the yard.
Forget your feelings, they're so sad!

Sensitivity is barred,
That's for the girls; don't get me wrong,
But boys must be well…hard.

Listen to my dribbling song:
You're a lad, you've got to score
Or dream about it all night long.

Girls are goals, that's what they're for.
So if you want to be my mate,
And not some wimpish bore,

Embellish and exaggerate
Under pressure from your peers.
Above all, learn to cultivate

A total lack of tears.
Now I stagger like my dad,
Through all the blinding years,

Drunk, divorced, but I'm not sad
Though life's become well…hard;
This is how to be a lad,
I learned it in the yard.

Andrew Fusek Peters

Mid-term Break

I sat all morning in the college sick bay
Counting bells knelling classes to a close.
At two o'clock our neighbours drove me home.

In the porch I met a father crying –
He had always taken funerals in his stride –
And Big Jim Evans saying it was a hard blow.

The baby cooed and laughed and rocked the pram
When I came in, and I was embarrassed
by old men standing up to shake my hand

And tell me they were 'sorry for my trouble'.
Whispers informed strangers I was the eldest,
Away at school, as mother held my hand

In hers and coughed out angry tearless sighs.
At ten o'clock the ambulance arrived
With the corpse, stanched and bandaged by the nurses.

Next morning I went up into the room. Snowdrops
And candles soothed the bedside; I saw him
For the first time in six weeks. Paler now,

Wearing a poppy bruise on his left temple,
He lay in the four-foot box as in his cot.
No gaudy scars, the bumper knocked him clear.

A four-foot box, a foot for every year.

Seamus Heaney

PMT

The whole world's a headache
And I move through it
Like I'm wading through glass syrup
Even thought's slowed down
You speak   *Pause*
I hear you   *Pause*
The words shuffle themselves into a meaning.   *Pause*
The sense is in there somewhere
Like raisins in a cake. Pick, pick,
Pick the sense out.   *Pause*
And if I move too quickly
I'll burst that bubble that I'm moving in
Don't hassle me
Don't push
If I stay still and slow
That headache
That has the world so firmly in its grip
Will let me go.

Jan Dean

The Can-Can

When I dance
my blood runs like a river can
my feet fly like the birds can
my heart beats like a drum can.
Because when I dance I can, can
do anything
when I dance.

Flying over rooftops
I see my town below me,
where everybody knows me,
where all my problems throw me,
where heavy feet can slow me
But nobody can, can
stop me
when I dance.

My blood runs a race.
My feet fly in space.
My heart beats the pace.
Because when I dance I can, can
do anything
when I dance.

Mandy Coe

When Words

What I really need is to talk,
but a fist has made its home in my
throat while everyone round me
mouths death with nightmares
ganging curses on their tongues.

What I really need is to talk,
but the room is so dense with fear
that each gulp grips till I gasp
and burn in silence for tears
that beats this drum in my head.

What I really need is to talk,
but my ghost gets caught off guard
and though the smiliest child
peers back the laughter I'm
drowning inside is a trap.

What I really need is to talk,
but these lips clog over and sing to
themselves instead a song of inexplicable
hope for the day when words will
unleash on me finally like love.

But what I really need is to talk.

Anthony Wilson

Out, Damn –
Spot

New clothes.
Jewellery, shoes.
New hair style.
Can't lose.

A pocketful
of cash is clever.
This'll be
the best date ever.

Hope she knows
how lucky – Oh, no!
Suddenly
I'm Quasimodo.

Can't be true.
Gross, or what?
On my chin –
there's a spot!

Jill Townsend

Gone Away

Luella leans on walls and weeps.
She's young and plain, with hopeless eyes
and owning nothing in the world
but skimpy clothes and bitten nails.
Weak webs of hair spin round her face
and thin, bruised arms hang limp like string.
Her sad soul flutters out of doors.
Above, bent branches twitch and grate,
they tamper with the evening sky
which darkens heavily in drifts.
Thin shining wires trail swaying loops
across the night, while voices call
from phone to phone, but no-one cares
enough to wonder what she does.
The evening star is made of paste
and cold grass grows in empty parks.
She's run away and hides in fear
of folk at home and men in cars.
She thinks that everything's her fault.
Her days are long and nights are worse.
She only has herself to sell
and soon there will be nothing left.

Jenny Morris

Triolet

(After *Triolet* by Wendy Cope)

I used to think that boys were all moronic.
Strange – I know it wasn't long ago.
My smug and supercilious scorn were chronic.
I used to think that boys were all moronic.
But now my boyfriend's kiss is supersonic
And we relish smoochy clinches, long and slow.
I used to think that boys were all moronic.
Strange – I know it wasn't long ago.

Penny Kent

5.Fancy You or Fancy Free?

57

Within Spitting Distance

Pucker those lips, prepare to dive,
Brush those teeth 'til they feel alive
Take a breath, fill up your lungs,
Ready for the race of teenage tongues,
Round and round like a washing machine,
Until you encounter Nick-O-Teen:
By gum, it's time to stop and think
And ban his brain-dead, bad-breath stink.
Admit it girl, it wouldn't go far,
Chuck him out and say tar-tar!
The race is lost, this boy's a mutt,
Who wants to snog a cigarette butt?

Polly Peters

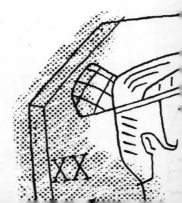

Cerinthus Is Unfaithful

I am glad you think you can get away with this
Allowing yourself a liberty at my expense -
That a togged-up tart with a wool basket
Is worthier of your attentions than Sulpicia
Daughter of Servius though she be.
Others care about me and are indignant
On my behalf that I must give place
To a low-born bit of stuff such as she is.

Sulpicia, Roman Poetess (1st century BC) Aged 15
Translated by John Heath-Stubbs

This Kissing Business

Should I part my lips, or pucker?
Bite them tightly? Blow or suck or

hold my breath? Perhaps I'll practise
on my mirror. See, the fact is

I'm not sure what is expected
when four lips become connected.

Gina Douthwaite

Say Cheese

(After Shakespeare's Sonnet No 18)

Shall I compare you to a plate of cheese?
You made me crumble, turned my heart to jelly,
Oh I had a case of trembling knees,
For Barry, the big cheese (somewhat smelly)
Just listen bud, don't call me darling, eh?
I'm not totally dim though you melted my heart
I saw you snog Samantha on Sunday,
I'm so cheesed off, it's time for us to part!
Your cheesiness will never fade,
Though I admit you had me in a pickle,
Nor shall you brag that I was betrayed
Barry, so un-mature and fickle
So long as girls have brains to stop and think
They'd say you're a moron and you stink!

Andrew Fusek Peters

Sonnet XVIII

Shall I compare thee to a summer's day?
Thou art more lovely and more temperate:
Rough winds do shake the darling buds of May,
And summer's lease hath all too short a date
Sometime too hot the eye of heaven shines,
And often is his gold complexion dimm'd:
And every fair from fair sometime declines,
By chance, or nature's changing course, untrimm'd;
But thy eternal summer shall not fade,
Nor lose possession of that fair thou owest;
Nor shall Death brag thou wander'st in his shade,
When in eternal lines to time thou growest;
So long as men can breathe, or eyes can see,
So long lives this, and this gives life to thee.

William Shakespeare

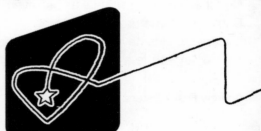

Official Report

The lads asked if I'd kissed her yet.
"What was it like?"
"Come on, Mike."
I felt kind of difficult. *Sort of wet,*
nothing to mention,
you know." "But French?"
"Of course. She really wanted it."
"What, all the way?
What did she say?"
"We snogged and played around a bit."
"What did you do though?"
(We played Cluedo)
"And where?" (It was in the lounge with her sister
there, and her brother,
her dad and her mother.
And that's the main reason I haven't yet kissed her.)

Jill Townsend

Sonnet From The Portuguese XLIII

How do I love thee? Let me count the ways.
I love thee to the depth and breadth and height
My soul can reach, when feeling out of sight
For the ends of Being and ideal Grace.
I love thee to the level of everyday's
Most quiet need, by sun and candlelight.
I love thee freely, as men strive for Right;
I love thee purely, as they turn from Praise.
I love thee with the passion put to use
In my old griefs, and with my childhood's faith.
I love thee with a love I seemed to lose
With my lost saints – I love thee with the breath
Smiles, tears, of all my life! – and, if God choose,
I shall but love thee better after death.

Elizabeth Barrett Browning 1806-61

How Do I Dump Lee?

(after *Sonnet from the Portuguese XLIII* by Elizabeth Barrett Browning)

How do I dump Lee? Let me count the ways.
I'll dump Lee with a gentleness that spites
the nose on my face. Or with lies so white
they speak of needing space, and mates. Or say
I'll dump Lee with an honesty display
so true. But, *I don't love you*, just don't seem right.
I'll dump Lee, with a *texie* late tonight.
I'll dump Lee, with *I think I might be gay!*
I'll dump Lee, with the need to love and lose,
leave out, he's so boring. Then pause for breath,
I'll dump Lee, with a really good excuse
such as, my death! I'll dump Lee is all that's left,
his spots, and his cute bott's not what I choose.
I shall dump Lee, instead of his mate Jeff.

Sheenagh Collins

67

Asking Out

I'd love to ask her out.
But how to go about it
is the thing.

Do I say,
'Fancy the cinema on Saturday?'

What if she says,
'Yes I do but not with you!'

Do I reply,
'That's ok.
I heard it's a rubbish film anyway!'

Then what if it gets round
she turned me down?

It isn't worth the risk.

And it would be just as big
a mess if she says,
'Thanks. The answer's yes!'

What do I talk about?
I guess football and kick boxing's
out. What do you talk about
with girls?

Should I try to hold her hand?
What if my hands are sweaty,
or my armpits or my feet?

How do you snog?
What if I've got bad breath.
How can I tell?

Is breathing into your hand
any sort of test?

Things might be much simpler,
it seems to me, if we practised this
sort of stuff in PSHE.

Jim Hatfield

Reading My Neville

You know that old saying which starts
You can't judge a book... ?
Well this is how my parents read my boyfriend Neville.

He's a catalogue of disaster,
He's a childish comic,
He's a trashy saga heading for an unhappy ending,
He's a hedunnit,
He's a textbook villain
who should be kept well out of the reach of impressionable girls.

But here's how I read my Neville.

He's one eventful chapter after another:

scary,
hilarious,
romantic,
mysterious,
eye opening
and never boring.

It's true he's not my usual choice of a boyfriend
but having checked him out
I find my Neville's very hard to put down.

Philip Waddell

Teenage Foil

It's really a pity
my girl friend is pretty,
for when we are out
I'm left in no doubt
that she is the beauty.
For her it's a duty
to take what she needs.
She always succeeds.
We hunt as a twosome
but boys find me gruesome.
My face, plain and neat,
is made for defeat.
She's sharp and she's witty
and mocks my self-pity.
If only she'd lots
of pustules and spots.
I'd love her so smugly
if she could be ugly.

Jenny Morris

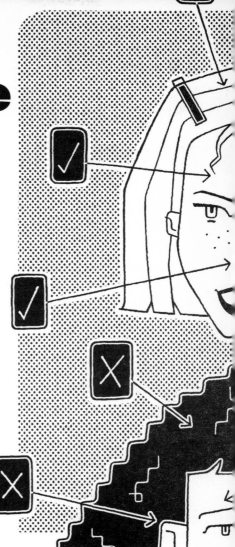

The House Is Not The Same Since You Left

The house is not the same since you left
the cooker is angry – it blames me
The TV tries desperately to stay busy
but occasionally I catch it staring out of the window
The washing up's feeling sorry for itself again
it just sits there saying "What's the point, what's the point?"
The curtains count the days
Nothing in the house will talk to me
I think your armchair's dead
The kettle tried to comfort me at first
but you know what its attention span's like
I've not told the plants yet
they still think you're on holiday
The bathroom misses you
I hardly see it these days
It still can't believe you didn't take it with you
The bedroom won't even look at me
since you left it keeps its eyes closed
all it wants to do is sleep, remembering better times
trying to lose itself in dreams
it seems like it's taken the easy way out
but at night I hear the pillows
weeping into the sheets.

Henry Normal

Er

Seen it in the toilets
written on the wall
who does what and how with who

but I can't believe it's all
truthful, honest or correct -
especially the bit on you

screaming in red felt-tip
among the sneers and boasts -
tried to scrub it with my sleeve.

Diagrams scratched on the door
explain the body thing but miss
out what worries me the most;

my awkward silence when we meet
tongue-tied in the corridor:
no words on the walls suggest

ways to be friends - and before
any touch of hands or lips
it's words I'm groping for.

Dave Calder

Too Late To Spell It Out

P ushed his hand off my knee.
R an his hand up my thigh.
E dged my body away,
G ave a gasp not a sigh.
N o - I strained in his ear
A nd *No* was my intent,
N ow he tells me he thought
T hat *Yes* was what I meant.

Philip Waddell

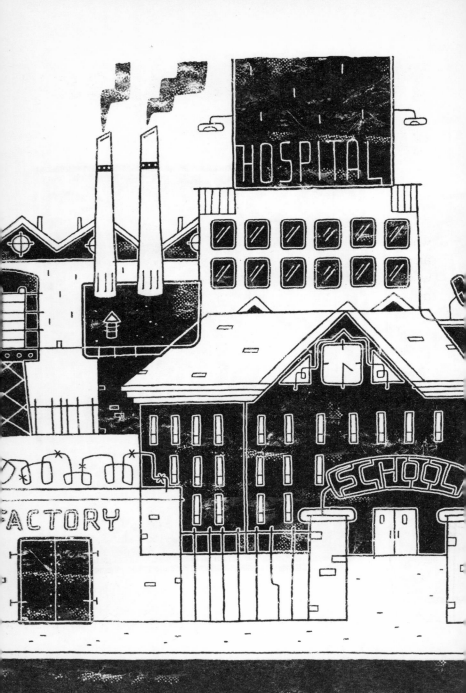

The Three Ages Of Mam

No more school.
A baby is cool.
They'll know who I am
when I'm pushing a pram,
and people will stop
when I go to the shop
and ask for a peep
at the baby asleep.

It's half past four.
How much more?
She's cried all night
and I'm knackered, right?
And now I bet
she's hungry and wet,
but I just can't keep
this up with no sleep.

They're taking exams
now at school. The pram's
broken. The baby
needs clothes. Maybe
I'll get a job.
But I look a slob.
No qualifications.
Kept by relations.
If I just had some money!
But this isn't fun -
being stuck in this heap
with no friends. And no sleep.

Jill Townsend

Alma Mater

Earth disturbs; no sleep
stills churchyard where a verger's eye
notes troubled soil. He ungrounds
a sports bag, biro scrawled.
Unzipping spills two toys,
one soft ET to cuddle, and one stiff;
a rigored son, towel blanketed.

But no heaping of clay could extinguish the fire
When Adam and Eros and Don Juan conspire,
So don't turn your thoughts from this child's agony
For she could have been you, sister, could have been me.

Schoolfriends who giggled
at pen-named names
voice an identity. She
bears stigmata on a body
distanced a mere decade and a half
from her own mother's womb.

And the blood in her tears cannot be unstained,
And the wrench in her gut will not be explained,
And a lifetime's too short for her life's misery,
And she could have been you, sister, could have been me.

Nurse, teacher, parent
wonder how she
could know and count, conceal
the swell that swallowed up her childhood.
Exam texts beckon. Pythagoras
makes rules. Babies
are biology fixed in year ten.

And a life has been traded for living hell dreams
of a tiny blue doll and his moment-hushed screams.
And GCSE turns ET, R.I.P.
Yes, she could have been you, sister, could have been me.

Alison Chisholm

Birthday Treat

Out for a January birthday celebration
in the homely but free
embracing fug of a welcoming pub
the gang of lads drank round after round,
got plastered,
and mixed the birthday boy an entertaining cocktail
of strong percent proofs
which he laughingly swigged down,
acting the clown.
Later, on the way home, roofs swung askew
and buildings swayed and bulged like earthquake visions
in the blur of his unhinged eyes.
When the street whirled
and he fell to the stone cold pavement
the lads around him giggled helplessly,
flung arms across one another's shoulders in fuddled sympathy
and stumbled away towards their beds of oblivion.
Too drunk to comprehend his plight,
they simply abandoned their now uninteresting friend
to the intimate embrace of the freezing winter night.

A police patrol found him lying there still stupefied,
the alcohol coursing through him like a poisonous tide.
In hospital the doctors pumped his stomach out.

Without that, they said, he would probably have died.
Strangely, when his parents were called,
the mother, furious, raged and swore.
It was his father who cried.

Penny Kent

Glue

I have bought glue to stick together
What has fallen apart. Foul weather
Lends this concrete car park
A backdrop of dripping dumb down dark.
Time dawdles its frantic feet, drags
As we suck on plastic shopping bags
Breathe the fume that burns the brain.
Oblivious now to the singing rain,
We stagger down the echoing well
Under the weight of the sickening spell
Where clouds have stuck the sky together,
And broke our hearts in this foul weather.

Andrew Fusek Peters

What's The Problem?

So many people getting into drugs –
Can't think what's the matter with them all.
If I feel low, things get too much,
I take a nice walk round the shopping mall.

Of course, I blame the parents, and the teachers,
– lack of proper discipline and care.
It wouldn't hurt to bring back National Service…
I don't suppose you'd have a fag to spare?

They ought to be content with what they've got.
What is it that they're wanting to forget?
No stimulants – a brisk walk does for me –
down the Bookies for my daily bet.

Police and courts should all take tougher measures.
They need a short, sharp shock, that's what I think!
You don't need all that stuff to get through life –
but, stone me, I could use another drink.

Tony Lucas

Fags...

"I'm thirty down to three. . .

Not bad,"

...she says...

Twenty-seven, I think to myself.
I was always good at sums,
thanks to Mr Rogers
(my sum teacher)
who sadly
smoked himself to death.

Peter Dixon

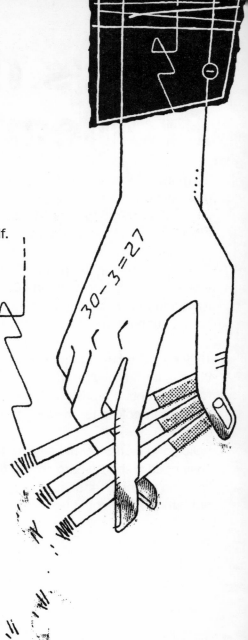

Drug Abuse

You stinking, stupid, useless pea-brained drug!

Mike Jubb

Silver Needle

Silver needle,
bring me comfort.
Silver needle,
bring me bliss.
Silver needle,
ease my sorrow.
Soothe me with
your silver kiss.

Silver needle
worked its magic,
filled me with
its silver breath.
Silver needle's kiss
was tragic,
killed me with
its silver death.

Tony Mitton

Bogeyman

On the corner stands a man
That everyone knows by sight,
And in his hand, a lager can
That turns his day to night.

The sun is shining bright,
For him, it's started to sink,
His mind a foggy twilight,
Filled with darkening drink.

If only he could stop and think
And throw away the can,
But all day long, like a statue,
On the corner, stands a man.

Andrew Fusek Peters

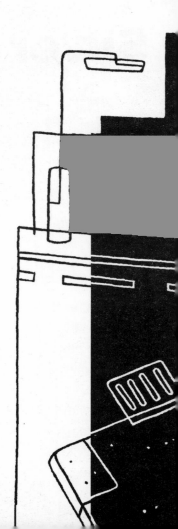

The Spark

When my dad lost his spark,
And cut the current of life
I was bereft, left in the dark.
with a gap no wire could cross.
I lived with loss
Until the day I had a joint. The zing
Was electric, amazing;
Switched on by dope
No longer a weed, grass gave me hope
And such a high
Like lightning I cracked the sky.
Made connections,
Sniffed out new directions;
I was a virgin in this drug relationship;
Shocked by my first acid trip,
The voltage was direct.
Fell in love with the vision effect.
Speed
Snatched my shyness. We agreed
That though it made our noses numb,
And comedown was a bummer,
It was fab,
Clothing that grey, drab
World in a sharp edged snow.
How long could it go
On for?
I wanted more, and more
Until the spark was spent

And I went mental.
Call it a teenage powercut.
My muddled mind shut
Down. Got paranoid, thought bombs would drop,
Fumbling in fear of the dark, couldn't stop
Crying.
At the age of sixteen, knew I was dying.
The chemicals I had adored
Led to the psychiatric ward.
Pumped me full of Largactil
Until the flicker of synapse was still.
I still remember to this day
How, overnight, my mother's hair went grey
I had burned the candle at both ends
And found out how shallow my friends
Were. None came,
Too busy in their own addictive game.
I came through,
Somehow grew
Up
The days and nights of throwing up were done
I had my fill of frantic fun.
At last, retired from getting wired...
And the moral? It's up to you.
Falling for crumbling rock,
There are other ways to get that shock...
Life, love, laughs, each day makes its mark
In the singing of the spirit's spark.

Andrew Fusek Peters

All Nite Disco

     Against
       knife-like lights my eyes peel like ripe plums
and the white strobe is timed to make you vomit.
Death sounds shriek and squeal to the wild, bucking floor,
amoebas of paint coagulate on walls
and, yes, we move on the bed of some rank pond.

     The girls
       joggle bodies in isolation,
faces stabbed as cut loaves, fingernails purpled
as if they've plundered damsons in the 'Ladies'.
Disorientation's the pain of the game
and as a torture room this takes some beating.

     The men,
       sidling like weary hunters, stalk flesh
while I grip a drink and cling to the swamped bar.
Cosmic with noise the ceiling aches to faint
as someone flops from a chair like a wet sack.
The groovers, stoned on sound, lurch towards dawn.

     Outside,
       the night's hard dreams
       fall to the streets
       as rain.

Wes Magee

Belonging

They call me gypsy,
trying to put me down.
Thinking I have no right
to be on their patch;
at their school, in their town.

You don't belong here,
they say to me.
You come and go.
You have no history.

We had a school topic—
Trace your family tree.

Most of the class went
back two generations.
Some three, to great-
grandparents.

I asked my mother,
Where did I come from?
We spent an evening
around the table in the
caravan.

We worked out my
family tree back to 1643.
In the stakes of belonging,
where does that leave me?

Jim Hatfield

Citizen Of The World

when you are very small
maybe not quite born
your parents move
for some reason you may never understand they move
from their own town
from their own land
and you grow up in a place
that is never quite your home

and all your childhood people
with a smile or a fist say
you're not from here are you
and part of you says fiercely yes I am
and part of you feels no I'm not
I belong where my parents belonged

but when you go to their town, their country
people there also say
you're not from here are you
and part of you says no I'm not
and part of you feels fiercely yes I am

and so you grow up both and neither
and belong everywhere and nowhere much the same
both stronger and weaker for the lack of ground
able to fly but not to rest

and all over the world, though you feel alone
are millions like you, like a great flock of swallows
soaring or falling exhausted, wings beating the rhythm
of the wind that laughs at fences or frontiers,
whose home is itself, and the whole world it moves over.

Dave Calder

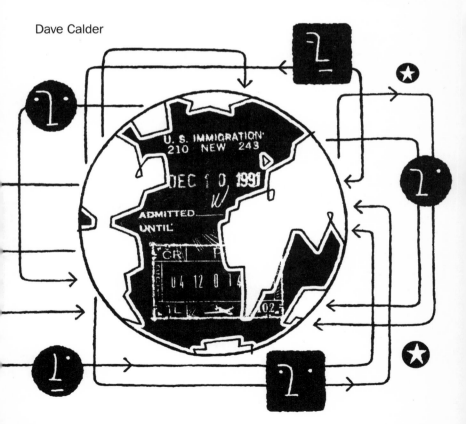

Race

Not much of an accident really.
Simple as staggering off a kerb
into the nearside wing of a number 22.

But the race was on
to urgent siren shriek
and keystone cops flicker
of blue against black

through street - casualty - blinding white corridor and lift - to theatre.

Later -
off his trolley -
he was sufficiently recovered to slur

'Don't let her touch me - that black one.'

Just as well really
no one could have told him
that the two units saving his skin
were vintage Jamaican.

Philip Waddell

Eurosceptic

Serbs, Czechs and Poles
are only good for filling holes.

Caribbeans and Asians.
How many more of these invasions?

Jews and Italians
upset the economic balance.

Hordes of Huguenots.
Who needs any more of those?

Castle-building Normans,
taxing everything that's poor men's.

Horny-headed Vikings,
so glad Britain's to your liking.

Road-building Romans -
the M1's static at the moment.

Gaels, Celts, you lot -
Do we want you? We do not.

Nobody about?
We only want foreigners out.

Some sheep. A few cave-dwellers.
Where are all the others, fellas?

Jill Townsend

The Professor Of Philosophy

We must stay! Said the student,
And more was learned in a day,
Than all his lean years.
Posters were printed for the people.
But soldiers were kingfishers,
Darting through dissent.
They were swift, and his friends not quick enough.
He had the luck of the minnow.

That night,
He smuggled himself back to his father's house,
And did not leave for five forgetful years.
His mother, the cookery tutor,
Was happy to store him in the larder.
The father fabricated false partitions,
And the hours were slowly consumed.

By day, his father scoured libraries
And stole his boy an education.
By night, he crept into the living room,
Stuffed blankets into the piano
And forged his silent sonatas.

The country stopped.
Eyes and lips were careful.
Neighbours could be more than instruments of gossip.
Borders grew tight as drums,
Beating out the rhythm of the east.

Five years fled, like refugees.
His teeth rotted for lack of pantry-visiting dentists.
The train dispatched father
Built a coffin out of card,
Laid it in a bed of coal
And soused it in vinegar to put dogs' noses out of joint.

His son folded himself into that dark envelope,
Without a kiss.

The lid was sealed,
And as the steam train shuffled slowly West,
He wondered if success would always smell so sour.

Andrew Fusek Peters

Extract from
Killing Time

Meanwhile, somewhere in the state of Colorado, armed to the
    teeth with thousands of flowers,
two boys entered the front door of their own high school
    and for almost four hours
gave floral tributes to fellow students and members of staff,
    beginning with red roses
strewn amongst unsuspecting pupils during their lunch hour,
    followed by posies
of peace lilies and wild orchids. Most thought the whole show
    was one elaborate hoax
using silk replicas of the real thing, plastic imitations,
    exquisite practical jokes,
but the flowers were no more fake than you or I,
    and were handed out
as compliments returned, favours repaid, in good faith,
    straight from the heart.
No would not be taken for an answer. Therefore a daffodil
    was tucked behind the ear
of a boy in a baseball hat, and marigolds and peonies
    threaded through the hair
of those caught on the stairs or spotted along corridors,
    until every pupil
who looked up from behind a desk could expect to be met
    with at least a petal
or a dusting of a pollen, if not an entire daisy-chain,
    or the colour-burst
of a dozen foxgloves, flowering for all their worth,
    or a buttonhole to the breast.

Upstairs in the school library, individuals were singled out
        for special attention:
some were showered with blossom, others wore their blooms
        like brooches or medallions;
even those who turned their backs or refused point-blank
        to accept such honours
were decorated with buds, unseasonable fruits and rosettes
        the same as the others.
By which time a crowd had gathered outside the school,
        drawn through suburbia
by the rumour of flowers in full bloom, drawn through the air
        like butterflies to buddleia,
like honey bees to honeysuckle, like hummingbirds
        dipping their tongues in,
some to soak up such over-exuberance of thought, others
        to savour the goings-on.
Finally, overcome by their own munificence or hay fever,
        the flower-boys pinned
the last blooms on themselves, somewhat selfishly perhaps,
        but had also planned
further surprises for those who swept through the aftermath
        of broom and buttercup:
garlands and bouquets were planted in lockers and cupboards,
        timed to erupt
like the first day of spring into the arms of those
        who, during the first bout,
either by fate or chance had somehow been overlooked
        and missed out.

Experts are now trying to say how two apparently quiet kids
        from an apple-pie town
could get their hands on a veritable rain-forest of plants
        and bring down
a whole botanical digest of one species or another onto the heads
        of classmates and teachers,
and where such fascination began, and why it should lead
        to an outpouring of this nature.
And even though many believe that flowers should be kept
        in expert hands
only, or left to specialists in the field such as florists,
        the law of the land
dictates that God, guts and gardening made the country
        what it is today
and for as long as the flower industry can see to it
        things are staying that way.
What they reckon is this: deny a person the right to carry
        flowers of his own
and he's liable to wind up on the business end of a flower
        somebody else has grown.
As for the two boys, it's back to the same old debate:
        is it something in the mind
that grows from birth, like a seed, or is it society
        makes a person that kind?

Simon Armitage

Tunnel Vision

on this suburban station
where the silence
never answers back

an illiterate spraycan
hisses hate
in a canister of gas

the NF slogan capitals
slide as bold as cowardice
across the face
of the sign that reads
LIMITED HEADROOM

Dave Ward

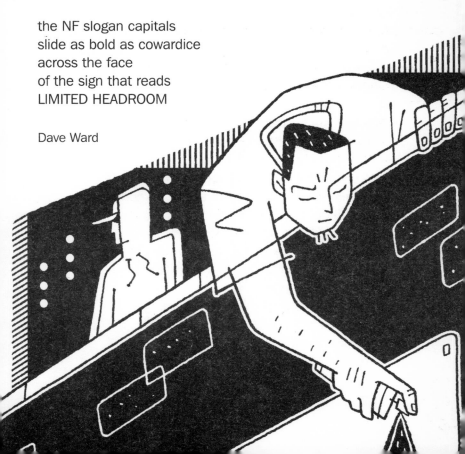

Half caste

Excuse me
standing on one leg
I'm half-caste

Explain yuself
wha yu mean
when yu say half-caste
yu mean when picasso
mix red an green
is a half-caste canvas/
explain yuself
wha yu mean
when yu say half-caste
yu mean when light an shadow
mix in de sky
is a half-caste weather/
well in dat case
england weather
nearly always half-caste
in fact some o dem cloud
half-caste till dem overcast
so spiteful dem dont want de sun
pass
ah rass/
explain yuself
wha yu mean
when yu say half-caste
yu mean when tchaikovsky
sit down at dah piano

an mix a black key
wid a white key
is a half-caste symphony/
Explain yuself
wha yu mean
Ah listening to yu wid de keen
half of mih ear
Ah lookin at yu wid de keen
half of mih eye
an when I'm introduced to you
I'm sure you'll understand
why I offer yu half-a-hand
an when I sleep at night
I close half-a-eye
consequently when I dream
I dream half-a-dream
an when moon begin to glow
I half-caste human being
cast half-a-shadow
but yu must come back tomorrow

wid de whole of yu eye
an de whole of yu ear
an de whole of yu mind

an I will tell yu
de other half
of my story

John Agard

102

Homelessness

in the middle of the street
in the middle of town
at midnight
he is scraping
a piece of chewing gum
from the tarmac

he moves methodically
stooped in the glare -
staring back at the headlamps
of swooping cars

picking up paper
picking up fagends

he searches the gutter
numb fingers scrabbling
at the dead leaves & sweet wrappers

looks up at his audience
shuffling in the doorway
of the hamburger cafe

"i've come to
clean up your town"
he says

Dave Ward

Anne Frank Kept A Dairy

Anne Frank kept a dairy.

Now in any normal farm the animals
in a dairy would be allowed to roam free
in the pasture meadows, so that
they could eat fresh grass, feel the west wind
and the drizzly rain on their backs.
With all that healthy freedom
they'd give the farmer good produce.

But in Anne Frank's dairy all the animals,
the cows and the bulls, the calves,
were caged in a tiny, airless attic.

This was not because Anne Frank was cruel:
no, it was because an evil farmer
stole Anne Frank's land and wouldn't let her
keep her animals in the countryside.
The evil farmer threatened to kill her animals.
So she hid them away in the attic of a farmhouse
where no-one would find them.

Day on day, the animals had to keep quiet
in case the evil farmer heard them.
The young calves and foals weren't allowed

to play chase or run-around games.
The grown-up animals were not allowed
to play music or to dance the tango
they danced so well.

The animals spent the time whispering I-spy,
playing chess and reading books.
You'd never hear a sound from that attic.
Not a shout, not a sneeze, not a sigh.

But eventually it was discovered
that there was a herd of animals
living cooped up in that attic.
The evil farmer had them all forced out -
some of them he sent to the slaughter-house
and some of them he starved in the poorest fields.

Even those young animals that were left alive
were too frail to play chase or run-around games.
The grown-up animals were still forbidden
to play music or to dance the tango
they danced so well.

We know all this because Anne Frank kept a diary.
But even if she had kept a *dairy*,
the truth would remain the same.

John Rice

Golden Shoes

Young Shona always wears her golden shoes
when she goes out. Such razzle-dazzle flash
will catch the wandering gaze of passing youths.
Those four-inch heels and glossy spangled toes
are clearly snares (make her feel bad and good).
At home the hairy slippers will suffice.
When she goes out she sometimes ties a wide
black velvet ribbon round her sallow neck.
Her mother scoffs, "You're like a munching cow
that's reaching out across a prickly hedge.''
But Shona doesn't care, just chews more gum
and shines the shoes that won't be mentioned once.
She thinks of boys who'd twirl and dance towards
her down the avenue of fantasy.
It's not like that in Percy Street where dead
old litter flaps against the terrace doors.
She's ready for her outing, but those shoes
are destined not to need so much repair.
Her wheelchair creaks as Shona turns to slam
the door. The golden prow sails down the road.

Jenny Morris

Author index

Acknowledgements

John Agard: 'Half-caste', from *Get Back Pimple*, published by Viking in 1996. By kind permission of John Agard.

Simon Armitage: Extract from 'Killing Time', published by Faber and Faber Ltd. By permission of Faber and Faber Ltd.

Clare Bevan: 'First Bra'. By kind permission of Clare Bevan.

Dave Calder: 'Arithmetic', 'Er' and 'Citizen of the world'. 'Arithmetic' © Dave Calder 1987, 'Er' and 'Citizen of the world'© Dave Calder 2000.

Alison Chisholm: 'Alma Mater'. First appeared in *Daring the Slipstream* (Headland 1997).

Mandy Coe: 'The Can-Can'. First appeared in *hot heads, warm hearts, cold streets,* published in 1996 by Stanley Thornes, editor John Foster. By kind permission of Mandy Coe.

Sheenagh Collins: 'How Do I Dump Lee?' By kind permission of Sheenagh Collins.

Jan Dean: PMT, © Jan Dean.

Helen Dunmore: 'If Only'. © Helen Dunmore.

Peter Dixon: 'Fags'. By kind permission of Peter Dixon.

Sarah Dore: 'Goodnight Kiss'. By kind permission of Sarah Dore.

Gina Douthwaite: 'This Kissing Business', first published in *Unzip Your Lips Again* (Macmillan Children's Books, 1999) © Gina Douthwaite. 'Cross words', published by Random House. By permission of Random House.

Jim Hatfield: 'Stammerer', 'Asking Out' and 'Belonging'. By kind permission of Jim Hatfield.

Seamus Heaney: 'Mid-Term Break' from *Death of a Naturalist,* published by Faber and Faber Ltd. By permission of Faber and Faber Ltd.

Mike Jubb: 'Too Much Like Hard Work', 'Haiku' and 'Drug Abuse'. By kind permission of Mike Jubb.

Penny Kent: 'Triolet', © 2001 Penny Kent. 'Birthday Treat', © 2001 Penny Kent.

Tony Lucas: 'What's the Problem?' Poems by Tony Lucas are published by Stride Publications: Rufus at Ocean Beach, 1999 and Too Far For Talk, 1990.

Wes Magee: 'All Nite Disco' by Wes Magee, from No Man's Land, by Wes Magee (Blackstaff Press, N.Ireland). © Wes Magee.

Kevin McCann: 'One Day in the Art Room' and 'Back at School'. By kind permission of Kevin McCann.

Ian McMillan: 'Quiet Kid On The Bus'. © Ian McMillan.

Tony Mitton: 'Silver Needle'. First appeared in hot heads, warm hearts, cold streets, published in 1996 by Stanley Thornes, editor John Foster. © Tony Mitton 1996.

Jenny Morris: 'Teenage Foil', © Jenny Morris. 'Gone Away' and 'Golden Shoes' first published in Urban Space, © Jenny Morris.

Andrew Motion: 'The Game'. Reprinted by permission of PFD on behalf of Andrew Motion.

Judith Nicholls: 'Lines'. © Judith Nicholls 1985, from Magic Mirror, by Judith Nicholls, published by Faber and Faber. Reprinted by permission of the author.

Brian Patten: 'The Minister For Exams', © Brian Patten. Published in 1996 by Flamingo in *Armarda.*

Polly Peters: 'Kid Story', 'Mr Rogers', 'My Mother', 'Get The Text Message' and 'Within Spitting Distance'. By kind permission of Polly Peters.

Andrew Fusek Peters: 'Hateboarding', 'Ballad of Matt the Knife', 'Leer Pressure', 'Say Cheese', 'Glue', 'Bogyeman', 'The Spark' and 'The Professor of Philosophy'. By kind permission of Andrew Fusek Peters.

David Petts: 'Some People's Words' and 'Family Break Up'. By kind permission of David Petts.

John Rice: 'Anne Frank Kept a Dairy', © the author 2001.

Roger Stevens: 'How Not To Pass GCSE Maths' and 'Head Teacher's Wise Words'. Both by kind permission of Roger Stevens.

Vernon Scannell: 'Inciendiary', by kind permission of the author.

Jean Sprackland: 'Fat', first published in *Tattoos for Mothers' Day* (Spike 1997).

Nick Toczek: 'Spots are cool'. Previously unpublished, copyright © Nick Toczek.

Jill Townsend: 'Out, Damn – Spot', 'Official Report', 'The Three Ages of Mam' and 'Eurosceptic'. © Jill Townsend 2001.

Philip Waddell: 'Doing Time', 'Race', 'Reading My Neville' and 'Too Late To Spell It Out'. By kind permission of Philip Waddell.

Dave Ward: 'Jambo Playing Football on the Back Field' from *Jambo* (Impact Books) 1994. 'Tunnel Vision' and 'In The Middle of the Street' from Tracts, (Headland) 1996.

Anthony Wilson: 'When Words'. First published in How Far From Here Is Home?' (Stride 1996) By kind permission of Anthony Wilson.

About the compiler:

Andrew Fusek Peters has been in working in education since 1987, performing and running poetry workshops. He has written over 30 anthologies, plays, storybooks and poetry collections. His anthologies include *Sheep Don't Go To School*, which the *Guardian* described as "The year's most innovative poetry collection." With Polly Peters, he wrote the bestselling and critically acclaimed teenage poetry collections *Poems With Attitude*. "It is rare and welcome to find a collection that speaks so directly to teenagers," wrote the *Guardian*. More information on Andrew's work can be found on **www.tallpoet.com.**